Travel Through
Japan

Joe Fullman

QEB Publishing

Copyright © 2007 QEB Publishing

First published in the United States by
QEB Publishing, Inc.
23062 La Cadena Drive
Laguna Hills, CA 92653

www.qeb-publishing.com

Library of Congress Control Number: 2007000943

ISBN 978 1 59566 357 3

Written by Joe Fullman
Designed by Chhaya Sajwan (Q2A Media)
Editor Honor Head
Picture Researcher Sujatha Menon (Q2A Media)

Publisher Steve Evans
Creative Director Zeta Davies
Senior Editor Hannah Ray

Printed and bound in China

Picture credits

Key: t = top, b = bottom, c = center,
l = left, r = right, FC = front cover

Badboo | **Dreamstime.com**: 4t, Index Stock Imagery/ **Photolibrary**: 4 background, 11m, Greg Elms/
Lonely Planet Images: 6–7t, 14b, Jtb Photo Communications Inc/ **Photolibrary**: 6b, 18b, 20b, 22t,
Science Photo Library/ **Photolibrary**: 7b, Bob Charlton/ **Lonely Planet Images**: 8b, Oliver Strewe:
9t, Michael S. Yamashita/**CORBIS**: 9b, Bart Parren/ **Shutterstock**: 10b, Martin Moos/ **Lonely Planet
Images**: 11t, Frank Carter/ **Lonely Planet Images**: 12b, **REUTERS**/Issei Kato: 13t, **REUTERS**/Eriko
Sugita: 13b, Mason Florence/ **Lonely Planet Images**: 14t, Frank Carter/ **Lonely Planet Images**:
15b, John Hay/ **Lonely Planet Images**: 16t, Brent/ **Lonely Planet Images**: 16b, 24b, John Ashburne/
Lonely Planet Images: 17t, Nordicphotos/ **Photolibrary**: 17b, Aflo Foto Agency/ **Photolibrary**:
19t, 25b, Mason Florence/ **Lonely Planet Images**: 19m, Jon Arnold Images/ **Photolibrary**: 20t, 23t,
21b, Ips Co Limited/ **Photolibrary**: 23b, Richard I'Anson/ **Lonely Planet Images**: 25t, **REUTERS**/
STRINGER Japan: 27t, Oliver Strewe/ **Lonely Planet Images**: 27b.

Words in **bold** can be found in the glossary on page 31.

Contents

Russia

China

La Pérouse Strait

HOKKAIDO

Sapporo

Aomori

Sea of
Japan

Pacific
Ocean

Akita

North
Korea

Niigata

Sendai

HONSHU

South
Korea

Japan

Matsue

Nagoya

Tokyo

Kyoto

Hiroshima

Osaka

Yokohama

Nagasaki

SHIKOKU

Philippine Sea

KYUSHU

Where in the world is Japan?

Japan is made up of a group of islands off the eastern coast of **Asia**. It is a very mountainous country, entirely surrounded by water. To the north is the La Pérouse Strait, the Sea of Japan is to the west, to the south is the Philippine Sea, and to the east is the Pacific Ocean. Its nearest neighboring countries are Russia, which lies across the sea to the north and northwest, and North Korea, South Korea, and China, which lie across the sea to the west. Taiwan lies to the southwest.

Japan is the world's 62nd-largest country, but has the world's tenth-largest population, with over 120 million people. Most of these people live in Japan's many cities.

Did you know?

OFFICIAL NAME: Japan

LOCATION: Eastern Asia

SURROUNDING COUNTRIES: Russia, North Korea, South Korea, China, and Taiwan

SURROUNDING SEAS AND OCEANS: La Pérouse Strait, Sea of Japan, East China Sea, Philippine Sea, Pacific Ocean

LENGTH OF COASTLINE: 18,486 mi. (29,750 km)

CAPITAL: Tokyo

AREA: 144,689 sq. mi. (374,744 sq. km)

POPULATION: 127,417,200

LIFE EXPECTANCY: Male: 76 years Female: 83 years

RELIGIONS: Shintoism, Buddhism, Christianity

LANGUAGES: Japanese

CLIMATE: Cool in the north, **temperate** in the center, **tropical** in the south. There's a **typhoon** season in September.

HIGHEST MOUNTAIN: Mount Fuji (12,388 ft./3,776 m high)

MAJOR RIVERS: Shinano (228 mi./367 km long), Tone (200 mi./322 km long)

CURRENCY: Yen

What is Japan like?

Japan is made up of many islands. There are over 3,900 of them in total. However, most of these islands are very small and do not have people living on them. Nearly all of the people in Japan live on just four main islands, which are named Hokkaido, Shikoku, Kyushu, and Honshu. Honshu is the largest island. More than 80% of the Japanese population lives here. This is where you will find the country's largest cities, including Kyoto and the capital, Tokyo.

Mountains and plains

As you travel around Japan, you'll see many mountains. Japan is filled with them. Over three-quarters of Japan's land is made up of mountain **ranges**. Everywhere you look, great towering peaks rise up into the sky. Most of the country's villages and cities have been built on flat **plains** between the mountains. Since there is so little flat land in Japan, Japanese homes are often very small and are built close to one another. Japanese cities are filled with **skyscrapers** that do not take up much ground space.

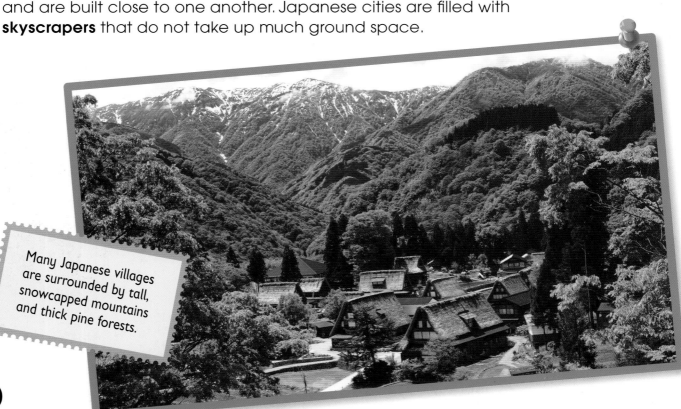

Many Japanese villages are surrounded by tall, snowcapped mountains and thick pine forests.

Earthquakes and volcanoes

If you were to spend some time in Japan, you might feel the earth shake. This is an earthquake, which are common in Japan. Most earthquakes are small and harmless. Every now and then, however, Japan is shaken by a large earthquake, which may topple buildings and cause giant cracks to appear in the roads. As you travel around, you may also see volcanoes oozing red-hot lava. Japan has many active volcanoes.

The latest gadgets

Most Japanese people live in cities. As you walk along the streets, you'll see shops selling lots of electronic gadgets, such as mobile phones, MP3 players, and video game consoles. Japan is famous for its electronic products, which it sells throughout the world. In Japan, trends, fashions, and technology change fast.

Japan's factories produce many electronic toys, such as this robot dog.

Different climates

Japan is a very long country, stretching for more than 1,864 mi. (3,000 km) from north to south. If you traveled from northern Japan to southern Japan, you would pass through a number of different climates. Hokkaido, the most northerly island, has very cold, snowy winters and cool summers. Honshu, Japan's largest island, has a milder climate. Farther south, the island of Kyushu enjoys mild winters and hot, humid summers.

Much of Japan enjoys hot summers during which fields of colorful flowers, such as these marigolds, come into bloom.

Cold winters, wet summers

If you spent the winter in Japan, you'd probably prefer to stay on the eastern side of the country. The winters there tend to be clear, dry, and mild. Winters on the western side of the country are much more fierce. The people who live there have to dress warm to protect themselves against bitterly cold winds blowing in from Russia and heavy snows. Japan's summers can be very wet, with many rainy days. In late summer, Japan is often hit by revolving tropical storms, known as typhoons. Typhoon winds can blow at up to 124 mph (200 kph). That's almost twice as fast as cars can travel on the highway! Typhoon winds can cause a lot of damage to buildings.

During the annual Sapporo Snow and Ice Festival on the island of Hokkaido, people carve giant statues out of ice.

During the rainy season in the summer, downpours are common and people carry umbrellas to stay dry.

YOU'VE GOT MAIL

Yokohama, where I live, is a port on the east coast of Honshu. In June, it rains almost every day. You have to wear plastic shoes and a raincoat to keep dry when you go out. When it has been raining a lot, the streets are filled with puddles, which are fun to splash around in. Sometimes the winds are very strong. Then, it can be difficult to walk and you have to stay indoors. When you look out of the window, you can see people's umbrellas being blown inside out by the wind.
Keiko

Up mountains and along rivers

The green-blue waters of Lake Okama fill the crater of Mount Zao, an **extinct** volcano on the island of Honshu.

Great ranges of snowcapped peaks run down the center of Japan. There are 15 mountains that stand over 9,843 ft. (3,000 m) high. Many of these are **dormant** volcanoes. This includes Japan's highest mountain, Mount Fuji, which stands at 12,388 ft. (3,776 m). Most of Japan's mountains are covered in thick pine forest.

Bridges and tunnels

As you travel around Japan, you will notice many bridges and tunnels. The country's villages and cities are often cut off from each other by mountains. Through the centuries, the Japanese people have built tunnels through the mountains and bridges over **gorges** to link the communities.

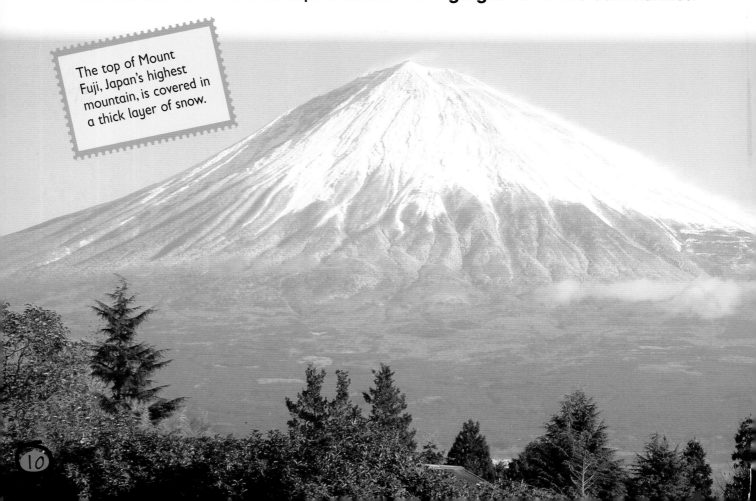

The top of Mount Fuji, Japan's highest mountain, is covered in a thick layer of snow.

Short rivers

Most of Japan's rivers begin in the central mountains and run down into either the Pacific Ocean to the east or the Sea of Japan to the west. Because Japan is very narrow, its rivers are not very long. (The longest, the Shinano, is 228 mi./367 km.) They are, however, steep and fast-flowing. After heavy rains, there is often flooding.

These Japanese macaques keep warm in winter by bathing in a natural hot pool near a volcano.

Shrinking lakes

Japan also has many lakes, some of which have formed in the craters of extinct volcanoes, such as Lake Towada on Honshu Island. The country's largest lake is Lake Biwa, also in Honshu. It is not as large as it used to be because the nearby cities of Kyoto and Osaka have used a lot of its water for drinking and for industry.

More than 60% of Japan is covered in forest. Many animals live here, including giant flying squirrels, macaques (a type of monkey), and wild boar.

Earthquakes, floods, and volcanoes

Japanese people have to be careful to avoid a number of natural hazards that affect their country. These natural events can cause a lot of damage, but the Japanese have learned to live with these dangers.

Earthquakes

Japan lies on a part of the Earth's surface where earthquakes are common. Every year there are hundreds of minor earthquakes. Most of these can barely be felt. However, every ten years or so Japan suffers a massive earthquake. The people take many precautions against earthquake damage. Their buildings are built so that in an earthquake, they will sway rather than fall down. As soon as an earthquake begins, electricity and gas supplies are cut off to prevent fire, and trains are automatically stopped from running. All Japanese schoolchildren learn earthquake emergency training.

A large earthquake can cause a lot of damage, blocking the streets with fallen rubble.

Volcanoes

Japan has over 60 active volcanoes. Many of these regularly send eruptions of red-hot lava spewing out onto the surrounding land. Though spectacular, Japan's volcanoes rarely cause much damage to property. The Japanese have learned to build their towns well out of the way of most eruptions.

Floods and landslides

Japan's most common natural hazards are caused by water. At the end of winter, melting snow in the mountains pours into rivers, which then burst their banks and flood towns and cities. In summer, heavy rains can cause landslides. This happens when soil on the side of a hill becomes waterlogged and heavy. Eventually, it gets so heavy that it slides down the hill causing a great deal of damage.

After a big storm, floodwater can quickly fill a city street, stopping cars in their tracks.

These children are practicing their earthquake drill. They have put on their protective hoods and are under their desks.

Once a month at school, we practice our earthquake drill. We're taught to get under our desks and hold on to its legs. We then put on hoods, which help protect us from falling rubble, flying glass, and heat, and file out of the classroom to the playground. There, the teacher takes attendance. We stand in the center of the playground away from the school buildings, which might fall down if there is a real earthquake.

Cato

At school

In Japan, children start school at the age of six. They attend elementary school for six years, and then go on to middle school for three years. These nine years of schooling are **compulsory**. After this, the children have the choice to go on to high school for another three years. Finally, if their grades are good enough, they can go to college for four years.

Baseball is very popular in Japan. Many schools have baseball clubs where children can practice their skills after their regular lessons.

May 5th is Children's Day in Japan, a national holiday to celebrate children.

Many Japanese children have to wear a uniform when they go to school.

Subjects

Japanese children are taught a wide range of subjects. At elementary school, students learn Japanese, math, science, history, geography, music, physical education, food technology, and information technology. Some students learn English, although this is usually only taught to older children. Students are also taught the traditional Japanese art of shodo—which is writing Japanese symbols using a brush and ink.

Activities

Outside of their official classes, children can also take part in a range of other school activities. They can play sports, such as baseball and soccer, or learn traditional Japanese crafts such as origami (paper folding) and ikebana (flower arranging). They are also taken on school trips to historical sites.

In the morning, we had math and Japanese lessons. Then we ate our lunch together in the classroom. The class is divided into a number of small groups. Each day, one group takes its turn to serve the others their food. In the afternoon, we had my favorite lesson—physical education. Then, we played baseball. Finally, we cleaned up the classroom together. We do this every day before going home.
Takumi

On a school trip, Japanese children will often wear brightly colored caps, so that they can be easily seen by drivers— and their teacher!

Crowded cities

Because there is so little flat land in Japan, the cities are filled with tall buildings, which take up less space on the ground.

Visit any Japanese city and there is one thing you're sure to see—people. Japan has the tenth-largest population in the world, with over 120 million people. Around 80% of them live in cities. Japan has 12 cities with a population of more than a million. Most of these are located on the east side of the country.

Close together

Japan has a very high **population density**. In other words, it is very crowded. There is only a small amount of space for people to live because of the mountains. On average, there are more than 880 people living in each square mile. In America, there are just 75 people per square mile.

Capital city

Tokyo is the capital of Japan and the country's largest city. It is also where many of Japan's most important businesses and government buildings are located. More than 12 million people live in the city center and more than 30 million in the Greater Tokyo Area—that's a quarter of Japan's population.

People fill the streets of Shibuya, one of Tokyo's most crowded districts, where there is a population density of more than 31,000 people per sq mi.

These children are reading manga stories, a type of comic book popular in Japan.

My name is Kenta. I live in an apartment in Tokyo, where I share a room with my brother, Naoki. At home, I like to play computer games and watch cartoons, called **anime**, on TV. Sometimes, I read **manga** comic books. When I'm out with my friends, I also like to play a traditional Japanese game called bei-goma. To play, everyone must spin a top at the same time. The person who gets their top to spin for the longest time wins the game.

Wooden houses

At the center of most Japanese cities, buildings tend to be made of steel and concrete. However, in the suburbs where the majority of the people live, houses are often built out of wood. Many Japanese houses have floors made of tatami (straw mats), which keep the rooms cool in summer and warm in winter. It is polite to remove your shoes when entering a Japanese home.

Japanese families traditionally sit on the floor around a low table to eat their meals.

Farming regions

As you travel around Japan, you'll see many farms, but not as many as you would have done in the past. Forty years ago, one in three people in Japan worked on a farm. Since then, Japan's **industries** have become very successful and many people have changed jobs to work in them. Today, only around one in 20 people still work on farms. Nearly all Japanese farms are situated on the country's flat plains.

Growing rice

The most important crop grown in Japan is rice, as it is the main part of the Japanese diet. Most of Japan's rice is grown on the main island of Honshu, on the Kanto Plain, the country's largest area of flat land. Rice is grown in flooded fields known as paddy fields. Japan's high rainfall helps the crop to grow well. Despite the country's small amount of farmland, Japan grows over 95% of the rice it eats.

These farmers are using modern farming equipment to plant rice in the huge paddy fields.

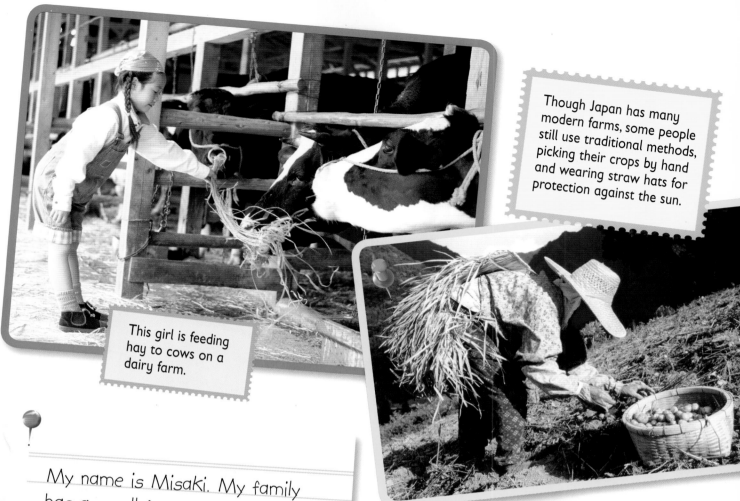

Though Japan has many modern farms, some people still use traditional methods, picking their crops by hand and wearing straw hats for protection against the sun.

This girl is feeding hay to cows on a dairy farm.

My name is Misaki. My family has a small farm on the island of Shikoku, where we grow a number of crops including rice, barley, tomatoes, and onions. My mother and father look after the farm during the week, but my brother and I help on weekends. Every week my father travels to the main island of Honshu to sell our vegetables at one of the big markets there. The farm doesn't make a lot of money, so we get a **grant** from the government to help us pay our bills.

Cattle and crops

There is very little good **pasture** in Japan. Most of the country's cattle are reared on the northern island of Hokkaido. The farms there supply much of the country's butter, milk, and beef. Barley is also grown there. To the south, on the hot, humid island of Kyushu, tropical fruits, such as mandarins and pineapples, are grown. There are also a number of tea plantations there. Throughout the country, Japan's forests are **logged** to supply timber for fuel, paper, and building materials.

Getting around

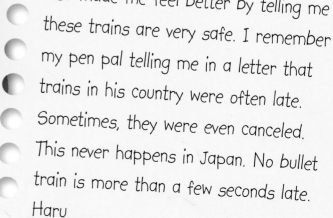

Japan's four main islands were once separated by stretches of sea, and people could only travel between them by boat or plane. However, in the past 50 years they have been linked together by a number of bridges and tunnels. Some of these are very long. The 34 mi. (54 km) Seikan Tunnel between Hokkaido and Honshu is the longest railway tunnel in the world. It is also the deepest, running 787 ft. (240 m) below the surface of the sea. The Akashi-Kaikyo Bridge between Honshu and Awaji Island is the world's longest **suspension bridge**, measuring 6,532 ft. (1,991 m).

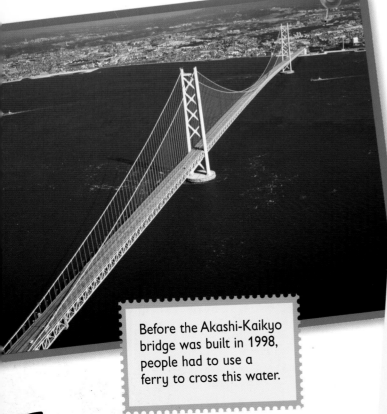

Before the Akashi-Kaikyo bridge was built in 1998, people had to use a ferry to cross this water.

Today I got the bullet train for the first time from Tokyo to Fukushima, where my aunt and uncle live. I was a little scared at first because I know the train travels very quickly and I thought I might feel sick. However, the train ride was very smooth. My mom also made me feel better by telling me these trains are very safe. I remember my pen pal telling me in a letter that trains in his country were often late. Sometimes, they were even canceled. This never happens in Japan. No bullet train is more than a few seconds late.
Haru

The long, streamlined nose of a bullet train helps it to move fast through the air.

Bullet trains

Japan's most famous forms of transport are its shinkansen, or bullet trains. These trains travel around the country at great speeds of up to 149 mph (240 kph). Long distances can be covered very quickly. The bullet train network was introduced in 1964. Since then, the trains have carried over three billion passengers.

Space to land

Japan's road and rail links are so good that few people use planes to travel around the country. However, Japan does have many visitors from other countries who travel in by plane. This used to be a problem because planes need a lot of flat space on which to take off and land. Mountain-filled Japan does not have much flat space. To solve this, the Kansai International Airport in Osaka Bay was built off the coast, on an artificial island in the middle of the sea. It is linked to the mainland by a bridge.

Kansai International Airport sits on a specially built, square-shaped island just off the coast of mainland Japan.

Food and drink

As you travel around Japan, you will be offered many different types of food. Wherever you go, however, you will be served rice. Rice is the main food of Japan and is eaten at most meals. In fact, the word for meal in Japan is "gohan," which also means rice. Because people in Japan use **chopsticks** to eat their food, their rice is usually cooked so that the grains stick together, which makes it easier to pick up.

Japan has many fish markets where people can buy the latest fresh catches.

My name is Tomoko. I live in Sapporo. At home, my favorite food is sukiyaki. This is a mixture of vegetables and meat cooked with a **soy sauce** and served with raw egg dip. When I'm out, I also like to try different foreign foods, such as hamburgers.

Lots of fish

The Japanese have more fishing boats and eat more fish than any other country on Earth. Fishing takes place all around the country's long coastline, as well as out at sea. Fish are also farmed in the country's inland sea, the area of water that separates three of Japan's four main islands, Honshu, Shikoku, and Kyushu.

Popular foods and drinks

There are a number of delicious foods that are common all over Japan. Miso is a mixture of soy beans and barley, and is often used to flavor soup. Sushi is another of the country's most famous foods—it is small pieces of cold rice, usually served with slices of raw fish, shellfish, and seaweed. Tempura is the name given to shellfish and vegetables that have been fried in a light, crisp batter. Green tea, served without milk or sugar, is one of Japan's most popular drinks.

In some sushi bars, customers can choose their dishes from a revolving conveyor belt.

A changing diet

The Japanese diet has changed a lot in the last 50 years. More meat, bread, and dairy products are now eaten. Many cities also have branches of Western fast-food chains, which are very popular, particularly with young people. However, most Japanese people still eat very healthily. Japan has the highest **life expectancy** in the world thanks to the healthy food that most Japanese people eat.

Traditional Japanese teacups do not have handles.

Japanese tea sets always have either three or six cups, but never four. Four is an unlucky number in Japan.

Religion

Shintoism and Buddhism are the two main religions in Japan. Many Japanese people follow both these religions.

Shintoism

Shinto is Japan's oldest religion. Shinto followers believe that everything in the natural world—every tree, every rock, every plant—has its own god. There are thousands of Shinto gods. It is common for Japanese people to have Shinto **shrines** in their homes where they say prayers. Shinto has no holy writings, no leaders, and no forms of group worship.

Buddhism

Buddhism was first developed in India and China, and later brought to Japan. There is no god in Buddhism. Buddhist teaching is about achieving peace through meditation, or deep thought. Buddhists believe in **reincarnation**. The city of Kyoto has over 1,600 Buddhist temples.

Kinkakuji, or the "Golden Pavilion," is an important Buddhist shrine. Built in 1397, it was rebuilt in 1955 following a fire.

Sport

In Japan, people enjoy traditional Japanese activities, such as sumo and judo, as well as modern international sports, including baseball and soccer.

Sumo wrestling

Sumo is a very exciting and popular type of Japanese wrestling. Sumo wrestlers face each other in a ring marked with a rope. To win, one wrestler must push the other out of the ring, or trip them onto the ground. Sumo wrestlers are very big. The biggest weigh more than 397 lbs. (180 kg). Wrestlers wear colored loincloths called "fundoshi." Top sumo wrestlers are big celebrities in Japan.

Sumo wrestlers stamp on the ground before each bout to try and scare off their opponents.

Judo

Like sumo, judo is a type of wrestling. The wrestlers try to throw each other onto the ground using different holds and moves. Judo is one of the sports performed at the Olympics. Judo wrestlers are much smaller than sumo wrestlers! They usually wear a white, loose-fitting top and trousers.

Kendo

Kendo is a type of sword fighting using wooden swords made from bamboo. Competitors wear masks and chest guards to protect themselves from getting hurt. To win, one opponent must strike the other on the head or chest with their sword.

Judo wrestlers wear a white uniform known as a judogi.

Industry and technology

Japan has the second-largest **economy** in the world, after the USA. If you were to walk through the center of a big Japanese city, such as Tokyo or Sapporo, you would see stores selling many different Japanese products. Japan also sells its goods to other countries. Many of its biggest companies are known throughout the world. Most Japanese industries are in the big cities on the Pacific side of the country.

High tech goods

Japan is perhaps most famous for its high tech goods—TVs, DVD players, digital cameras, and computer-game consoles, which are sold around the world. You probably have some Japanese goods in your house. See if you can find out what they are.

Nuclear power

Japan does not have many natural fuel reserves, such as supplies of coal or gas. Instead, it has to **import** these from abroad. Over 80% of Japan's electricity is made using fuels that have been bought from other countries. The other 20% is produced by 55 **nuclear power stations** that are spread around the country.

Nuclear power stations contain many harmful substances, which must be protected behind huge walls of thick concrete.

More and more people in Japan are training to become chefs.

Japan's cars are among the most advanced in the world.

Japanese workers

Fifty years ago, most people in Japan worked on farms or had jobs in heavy industries, such as iron and steel production. Today, the majority of Japanese people have jobs in the **service industries**, working in restaurants, stores, banks, and in leisure and tourism.

Activity ideas

1 Japan is made up of a group of islands known as an archipelago. Do an Internet search to find out about different archipelagos around the world, such as the British Isles. Do they have as many islands as Japan? How many of these islands have people living on them?

2 Use an atlas of the world to find other places on the same **latitude** as Tokyo, Japan. Using the Internet, find out if these other countries have the same amount of rainfall or the same average temperature as Japan, or if they differ. Plot the results on a chart to compare weather conditions in these countries.

3 Plan an imaginary trip around Japan. If you could visit just six places in Japan, where would you go? Why? How would you get to Japan? How long would it take you? How would you get to the different places in Japan?

4 Make a 3D map of Japan using papier-mâché. Look at the map of Japan on page 4 of this book and use it to copy the rough shape of the four main islands onto a sheet of cardboard. Crumple up pieces of paper and stick them over the shapes to build up the "land." Remember to make a lot of peaks because Japan has many mountains. Glue these firmly in place. Coat in PVA glue, and cover the whole model carefully with a sheet of tissue paper. Push the paper into all the inlets and coves you have created. Repeat this step until you have a smooth surface and leave it to dry. Then, paint and label your model.

5 Research and write a project on Japanese samurai warriors. Who were they? When did they live? How did they protect themselves?

6 Using the Internet, find out about the sort of clothes people wear in Japan. What was the Japanese style of dress in olden times? How do modern Japanese people dress? Draw and label a picture of someone wearing traditional Japanese clothes. Why do you think they wore clothes like this?

7 Search through cookbooks and on the Internet to find a recipe for some Japanese foods, such as sushi or sukiyaki. With an adult, cook the foods together, and create a pretend restaurant area where you can create menus and take turns being a waiter and diner, before eating the food. You could also buy some examples of different Japanese foods and taste them, and perhaps write reviews of the food. How do they compare to American foods? You could make a display of the reports of the food.

NOTE FOR ADULTS:
Please ensure that children do not suffer from any food allergies before making or eating any food.

8 Using the Internet and travel brochures, find the images and pictures of Japan most often shown to tourists traveling to the country. Print out the pictures to make a collage of "Tourist Japan." What are the most popular places in Japan? What ideas and images do travel Web sites use to sell Japan as a travel destination? Create a poster, encouraging people to visit Japan.

9 Look on the Internet and in your local library for books and information on origami—the Japanese art of folding pieces of paper into different shapes, such as animals, dinosaurs, flowers, and boats. Cut some paper into squares and try origami for yourself.

10 Make a fact file about the Seikan Rail Tunnel between Hokkaido and Honshu, the longest and deepest railway tunnel in the world. Afterward, you could make a working model. (You'll need a model train for this activity.) Make the tunnel by bending a sheet of thin cardstock and attaching it to a base—the side from a strong cardboard box will do. Paint the model with brown paint mixed with a little PVA glue for strength. Tear strips of blue tissue paper, crêpe paper, and cellophane in shades of blue, and stick them to the base beside the tunnel on either side—this will be the sea. You could even add clay sea creatures. When everything is dry, send your model train through the tunnel!

11 Imagine you are traveling across Japan, using its fast bullet trains to pass over bridges and through tunnels. Alternatively, imagine you are climbing one of the country's many high mountains. Write entries in an imaginary blog about your journey. What do you see? Who do you meet? Does anything funny happen to you? What do you discover about Japan?

13 See if your local library has any children's manga comic books. Make up a story and write it in a manga-style comic strip using colored pens and pencils.

12 Write a tourist leaflet describing a city in Japan. What does the city look like? What sort of buildings does it have? Remember to use language that will make people want to visit.

14 Carry out research on the Internet and in the library, and then write a report about sumo wrestling. What are the rules of the sport? How does one sumo wrestler beat another? What do sumo wrestlers wear? What do sumo wrestlers eat? How often are sumo competitions held?

Glossary

anime Cartoon programs shown on TV

Asia One of the seven continents that make up Earth's land. The others are North America, South America, Europe, Africa, Australia, and Antarctica

chopsticks Two thin pieces of wood used to eat food

compulsory Something that has to be done

dormant Inactive or asleep

economy Everything that has to do with the making, selling, and buying of goods

extinct Something which is no longer alive or active. A volcano that has stopped erupting is extinct

gorges Deep valleys with steep sides

grant A gift or loan of money

import Buying goods from other countries

industries Companies that make products

latitude Distance from the equator (an imaginary circle around the middle of Earth, shown on most maps)

life expectancy The average number of years a person is expected to live—which is influenced by their lifestyle

logged When many trees have been cut down. Logging is the cutting down of trees in order to sell them

manga Japanese comic books

nuclear power stations Places that make electricity using nuclear power

pasture Fields where farm animals, such as cows and sheep, live and eat

plains Large areas of flat land

population density The number of people living in a certain amount of land. If there are a lot of people, the place has a high population density

ranges Several groups of mountains

reincarnation Being born again in another form after death

service industries Industries that provides services for other people, such as an entertainment show or a meal in a restaurant, rather than goods, such as cars or TVs

shrines Small temples to a god or gods

skyscrapers Very tall buildings

soy sauce A dark brown sauce made from soy beans that is popular in Japan

suspension bridge A bridge on which the weight is supported by cables hung from high towers

temperate Mild weather that is neither too hot nor too cold

tropical Hot and humid, the climate of the Tropics—the areas either side of the equator

typhoon A severe storm with strong winds that blow in a circular movement

Index